MIRANDA  D0264893

Dear

There is always
someone watching
over you to make
sure you are all right.
You are always in
my thoughts. I love
you very much.

X X X X X

stick a photo of
you both here

Big Secrets
for not so
little girls

WEIDENFELD & NICOLSON

First published in Great Britain in 2007
by Weidenfeld & Nicolson
10 9 8 7 6 5 4 3 2 1

Text copyright: Miranda Shearer 2007
Design and layout: Weidenfeld & Nicolson 2007
Illustrations by David Broadbent
Cover design by Madeleine Harris

All rights reserved. No part of this publication may be
reproduced, stored in a retrieval system, or transmitted, in
any form or by any means, electronic, mechanical, photocopying,
recording or otherwise, without the prior permission of both
the copyright owner and the above publisher.

The right of the copyright holders to be identified as the
authors of this work has been asserted in accordance
with the Copyright, Designs and Patents Act 1988.

A CIP catalogue record for this book is available
from the British Library.
isbn-13: 978 0 297 84457 2
isbn-10: 0 297 84457 7

Printed and bound in Malaysia

The Orion Publishing Group's policy is to use papers that are natural,
renewable and recyclable products and made from wood grown in
sustainable forests. The logging and manufacturing processes are
expected to conform to the environmental regulations of the country
of origin.

editorial director Susan Haynes
Designed by Grade and Austin Taylor
Design assistance by Joanna Cannon and Justin Hunt
Edited by Jinny Johnson

Photographs
Corbis: page 59; Getty Images: page 16 top left, page 16 bottom
right (under flap), page 52; Kobal Collection:
page 16 bottom left; Robin Matthews: page 16 bottom right,
page 17 top left, pages 19, 21, 29, 55, 59 (under flap); Rex
Features: page 55; Miranda Shearer: pages 8–11.

While every effort has been made to trace copyright
holders, if any have been inadvertently overlooked,
the publishers will be pleased to acknowledge them
in any future editions of this work.

Weidenfeld & Nicolson
The Orion Publishing Group Ltd
Orion House
5 Upper St Martin's Lane
London WC2H 9EA
www.orionbooks.co.uk

To my naughty little sister,
for always being yourself.

'It is better to do something and regret it than regret not ever having done anything.'
TO A CERTAIN EXTENT!

'Do sober what you said you would do drunk. That way you will learn to keep your mouth shut.'

'We are all born mad but some of us remain so.'

'Don't go where the path may lead, go instead where there is no path and leave a trail.'

CONTENTS

PROLOGUE

WHAT
TO DO

PLEASE NOTE: Pigs will fly b4 I can tell u how to live your life. This book is not about that. It is just to give you some answers and help along the way.

WHEN YOU
DON'T
HAVE A CLUE....

There are so many situations I have been in when I've wished that I knew what I was doing. Boys, make-up, bank accounts, paying gas and electricity bills, sex — all the stupid stuff that you never realise is harder than you think until you are right in the middle of the problem. These kind of problems pound at your head until you sort them out, then you realise they weren't problems at all, but just silly things that you need to overcome as you grow up. They are part of growing up.

That awful situation when you want to snog a guy and you feel like an idiot. When you fancy someone and you don't want anyone to know, yet you want him to use his telepathic powers and realise you do actually exist. When you think the way you are doing your make-up looks cool, but you look at photos a couple of years later and you think — oh, my god, how did that blue eyeshadow and liquid eyeliner get there! If I told you how to do all this, you would miss out on the fun of trying it for yourself. But here are some suggestions for when you get stuck, some funny thoughts, how to deal with awkward situations, things people forget to tell you, and other bits and pieces that even I felt embarrassed about writing.

I started this book as a way of giving my little sister Charissa a bit of guidance, some common sense and I hope a lot of reassurance during the next stage in her life. From the age of 16 to 23 I think there is a lot of learning to be done and fun to be had, and sometimes at this age we think we are invincible. Life is not about playing with fire or being pushed into doing things with your peers that you don't feel safe doing. The essential things you should get from this book are inspiration, courage, a feeling that you want to make the next stage of your life amazing, and maybe — if you're lucky — a few kinky tips your mum never taught you!

Miranda X

SEE THE

Take a year out and go travelling.

Travelling is the most nerve-wracking thing I ever did but the memories are etched on my mind forever. You might need a break after school. I certainly did! You need to learn about things that school can't teach you, but maybe a fisherman in Peru or a street kid in Ecuador can. You need to leave home and go on an adventure before university. I wanted to find my identity, learn about my limits and grow up a little before I could get my head round more studying. Parents might not make it easy.

They worry that something will happen to you, that you might never come back, and that you are too young to go off into the big wide world. But sometimes you need to ignore them! I learnt a lot about life. I was desperate to see something different, taste new foods, be more independent, and discover the strange and wonderful things I'd seen in books. Go with a friend, in a group, or even on your own like I did. You're never really alone because there are so many travellers. Close your eyes and pick a country on the map. It's good to have something to look forward to while you're doing your A-levels.

WORLD

There is so much LIFE on this Planet

I went to South America and my experiences were some of the most eye-opening I've had.

It is the most enchanting place in the world and I think about my adventures all the time. Travelling marked my life in a way I could not have imagined. Being in a completely alien place sharpens your wits and makes you feel alive — you are on your own, having to survive.

THIS IS HOW I DID IT

It was much scarier than I make it sound. Leaving home is the weirdest thing I have done so far. One minute I am sitting watching Hollyoaks and the next minute I am on a plane for 13 hours with a bunch of weirdos that I have to get along with for the three months we are together.

I worked hard to be able to go away. I had five jobs and although I was living at home, it was difficult to save. It was depressing too. All my friends were either at university or travelling already. I was the only one out of my group of friends who took a gap year. They all wish they had done it now. You can take time after university, but it's not the same. You have other things to do, like paying back a student loan, and you lose out on graduate scheme opportunities, which are extremely important.

* Pick a place far away that fascinates you * Volunteer work is a good way to start. * Pack a rucksack. * Go on your own, you will meet loads of people. * If you pluck up courage to go, you will realise how easy it actually is to travel.

So, I was scared, homesick, nervous, excited, and too far away from England to get back. Seeing so many new things is an indescribable adventure. Photographs and travel programmes are far from what you feel when you are trekking through the most beautiful mountains and sunbathing on incredible beaches, or walking through market towns and tiny villages in the middle of nowhere. You eat strange foods, see bizarre animals and have some time away from your family and country. Going away made me realise how important it is to learn about who you are. Where better to do this, than in a totally unknown environment? So, have I managed to persuade you to take a year out?!

WELL, HERE ARE TEN THINGS YOU NEED TO MAKE SURE YOU DO BEFORE YOU GO AND WHILE YOU ARE THERE

*MAKE SURE YOU BUY a good rucksack. Berghaus are amazing — get the 65-litre version with an extra 15 litres for all the funky things you buy in markets.

*GO TO YOUR NURSE and go through what jabs you need against weird diseases. Get them done early. Some you need to have three months before you go.

*BUY A LEG WALLET. The waist wallets always get cut off you and stolen (a few traveller's cheques are handy).

*TAKE TWO PAIRS OF JEANS, a couple of sexy tops, a couple of T-shirts, walking socks and cheap cotton socks, a pair of flip-flops, a pair of trainers, a bikini, a big warm jumper, a sleeping bag and a cotton cocoon to put inside it to keep it clean. If you are going somewhere hot you may only need the cocoon. Go to a camping shop and get a platypus for water, a washing line and a universal plug for sinks and baths. Use a sarong as a towel, it dries quicker and is much lighter. YOU DO NOT NEED A LOT OF STUFF. You can buy it all there!

*GET A MAP and a good book on where you are going. Take a diary to write in.

*TAKE A CAMERA — and make sure you have plenty of batteries, memory, film or whatever.

*MAKE SURE PEOPLE KNOW where you are at all times. Do not walk anywhere on your own.

*TAKE SAFE TOURIST BUSES as much as you can.

*IF YOU GO OFF ON A TREK, LOCK UP your things in a safe in a hostel and take some money just in case.

*DO NOT THINK THAT BECAUSE you are in a foreign country you can behave how you want to and go crazy. Respect the people around you, and their customs as you are being observed. People get stupid and let their hair down when they travel, and end up getting into trouble or danger. Keep your wits about you.

Have an amazing time. Watch your back.

Keep your things on you at all times. Never put them down, as there is always someone waiting to catch out the dappy blonde tourist. Keep your wits about you more than if you were walking in the roughest part of London and you will be all right.

JOBS

earning money is always a good thing! I've always had a job — it's good having a bit of extra cash to spend on sexy underwear and to be able to spoil yourself from time to time!

Bars and restaurants are a good start, but there can be long hours, lots of time on your feet, cheesy music, smoke, drunken idiots and narky customers. Work in bars where people your age work, and not where you and your friends drink. The bars where you drink always look so cool, until you end up practically living there!

Also I met loads of amazing people from working in funky bars on the other side of town. You actually make another group of friends. If you are travelling, you might meet your next travelling buddy who suggests going somewhere you had in mind. I worked with a girl in Peru who I travelled with to Ecuador for a month, and we had a pretty crazy time.

Learn to deal with wasted, rude or angry customers, and give as good as you get, in the nicest or funniest way possible!

Words of Wisdom

* DON'T PUT YOURSELF in a situation you don't want to be in.

* DON'T LET PEOPLE take advantage of you. You are there to do a job, not personal errands for your boss.

* DON'T STAY in a job you are unhappy with. You could end up making yourself ill, worried, and lose all your self-confidence and sense of worth. You are the most important thing and you being unhappy is really not going to help you sort anything out.

* DON'T LET YOUR BOSS scream at you, or take personal issues out on you. The moment bosses behave badly you lose respect for them and it's difficult to treat them as your boss.

* DON'T LET THEM pay you a shit salary if you are worth more. Some bosses are tight-fisted people who have forgotten what it was like to start at the bottom and that you have living expenses looming over you. Having said that, wages are fixed for a reason and usually go up not down. If bosses realise you are valuable they usually reward you if you are doing a good job.

* DON'T SLACK, work hard and you'll be given more opportunities and more respect.

* DON'T BITCH about your bosses too much (unless they really are taking the piss and making you unhappy). Talk to them if you have any problems. They can only listen and say yes or no. If they don't understand you or your problems, then maybe the job just isn't for you and you are working in the wrong place.

* FIND SOMETHING you enjoy doing — it can't be that hard. I am so sick of meeting people who hate their jobs. Do not settle for just anything. Go to loads of interviews and make sure you get a chance to interview the employers a little bit too.

* DO NOT GET STUCK. If you are in a job you love and it turns sour, you get bored or you realise you would like to be doing something else, then do it. Life is too short to feel rubbish about yourself.

HE LOVES ME... HE LOVES ME NOT...

Boys
come in
all shapes
and sizes
like we do. You
may have heard
the saying men
are from Mars
and women are
from Venus. So
People think t...
is true, othe...
don't.

You think
your ideal
man is tall,
dark and
handsome, and
then end up pulling
a sexy bald guy
like I did.

What I do
know is that in
the end we are
all just a bunch
of weirdos trying
to survive on
this pretty odd
planet called
earth, and
most of us
don't want
to do it
alone.

In ... wha... ... all attracted
to ... f... ...ns. Some you can
... ...s, mental, physical
...al feelings we don't
...w much about. I believe
...s a l...

...big
...sually
... what size
...erson attracted to
...s all those things
...ould change if
...had enough
...ney for a
...rgeon. I
...k your
...and I
...ads of boy... ...don't
...re about that anyway. Learn
...ow to make up for it by being
sexy and confident and they
won't be thinking about
what you have or haven't
got. We all end up
attracting the right
Person at the right time, so don't worry if you
are single. It means the right Person hasn't come
along yet. Maybe you need to relax and get out
there, have fun with your friends and wait for him
to come to you.
Some boys think that they should do the asking.
I do not think for one second it matters who does
what. I am much more up for making something work if I do
the chasing. I like proving I'm a worthwhile girlfriend.
Watch out for the last boys at a party. They
usually make a cheesy last attempt at the end
of the night not to go home empty-handed.

MAP TO THE KEY TO ROMANCE

What I really wanted to do is a little section on being gay. You and I both know people who have come out, and some have had an easier time than others. You usually want to say it's about time too, when they finally sit you down and tell you that they're gay. It is such a difficult subject to write about because to me, being gay is no different to being heterosexual. You like someone, you are sexually attracted to them, why should it matter if it's the same or opposite sex? My guru for this book, Tara, said the only thing that sums it up are the words from Blur: 'Boys who like Girls who like Girls who like Boys who like Boys who like Girls who like Girls.'

(You wish! There is no key. It's hard work. You think you've got the answer and you haven't. It's different for every person in every type of relationship.)

It really is like a treasure hunt with a load of traps along the way.

Always should be someone you really love...
It should never be an issue. Don't make it one.

eww. You mean those Martians who smell. Those things we are usually attracted to but don't know what to say to them unless we are really drunk! And even then we make a fool out of ourselves.

Boys should surprise you. Only on Valentine's day is not good enough. They should be doing romantic little things that make you feel yummy all year round, just as you should do for them. Last year I pulled back my bedcovers and found hundreds of hand-cut red hearts

There is no such thing
BOYS as MEN!

Make sure he gives you a little bit of plain, old-fashioned love. Being a good kisser is a good start!

MAKE SURE HE DOESN'T WEAR THESE.

Make sure he gives you flowers.

a girl needs strawberries & champagne.

GRAN

17

SIMPLE THINGS ABOUT BOYS

MAKE SURE HE CAN MAKE A FEW GOOD DISHES.

*Boys like to have farting competitions in bed.

*Find a dish his mum cooks or that he loves and learn to cook it really well.

*Boys are pretty simple. As long as you pander to their needs from time to time they are happy.

*A boy's smell will attract you to him.

*If a boy treats you like shit, preserve your feelings and tell him to get lost. Don't hang around and end up resenting him, regretting wasting time with him and losing all self respect. It ain't worth it, girl.

*You can spend hours with your mates trying to figure boys out, but don't forget you are usually looking at them from a girl's point of view. They're not that complicated.

Eww. You mean those Martians who smell. Those things we are usually attracted to but don't know what to say to them unless we are really drunk! And even then we make a fool out of ourselves.

Boys should surprise you. Only on Valentine's day is not good enough. They should be doing romantic little things that make you feel yummy all year round, just as you should do for them. Last year I pulled back my bedcovers and found hundreds of hand-cut red hearts, all saying 'I love you. Sooo romantic!

There is no such thing as MEN!

BOYS

Make sure he gives you a little bit of plain, old-fashioned love. Being a good kisser is a good start!

MAP TO THE KEY TO ROMANCE

(You wish! There is no key. It's hard work. You think you've got the answer and you haven't. It's different for every person in every type of relationship.)

What I really wanted to do is a little section on being gay. You and I both know people who have come out, and some have had an easier time than others. You usually want to say it's about time too, when they finally sit you down and tell you that they're gay. It is such a difficult subject to write about because to me, being gay is no different to being heterosexual. You like someone, you are sexually attracted to them, why should it matter if it's the same or opposite sex? My guru for this book, Tara, said the only thing that sums it up are the words from Blur: 'Boys who like Girls who like Girls who like Boys who like Boys who like Girls who like Girls.'

It really is like a treasure hunt with a load of traps along the way.

Always should be someone you really love... It should never be an issue. Don't make it one.

Remember you are a one & only. Be mysterious, sexy & the belle of the ball. Sometimes leaving men wondering is a good thing.

But be sure to let him know you love surprises too.

Boys need a little training from time to time...start with washing up and breakfast in bed!

If he is neither spontaneous nor imaginative and if he doesn't surprise you, he is boring!

LOVE & HATE
AND A BIT OF SEX

You will love lots of people for lots of reasons. Love changes. Your love for one boy may be a totally different feeling of love to what you feel for another guy. Love grows up as you do. Love can hurt, as they say, and be confusing, cause mistrust, be amazing or unsuitable, or perfect for a time. Love can make you do stupid things, say yes when you mean no, be funny, and sad. You cannot make someone love you. You can make someone who loves you love you more or less. You never really know what you have done to make this happen. If your love is equal in a relationship then it's pretty perfect. Don't say 'I love you' too much, don't say it too little. Never regret saying it, but never feel you have to say it either. Love can make your world go round, but it can make you fall flat on your face in despair too.

Hate is a pretty strong feeling. You can't like everyone and not everyone is going to like you. Never hate the people you once loved. Laugh at the good times, or at that person in particular if it makes you feel better. Some girls you will hate, but they will hate you more if you ignore them. Act like you don't care and think about why they are like that towards you. It is usually because they are jealous or sad or maybe they want to be your friend or they just think they are too cool. Hate is a waste of time — it only makes you bitter. If you and a boy break up it will be the end of the world for a while. When you are with someone you will never imagine yourself with someone else, until the next one comes along! Also if people let you down there is usually a good reason. If not, don't hate them, just remember we are not all the same. Some people screw up.

IF YOU CATCH MY DRIFT

& sex

A VERY PRIVATE AND INTIMATE SUBJECT

If you are asked to do something you don't want to do, say NO. No one is going to lose respect for you or think that you are a loser, or that you are an ice maiden — as most blokes kindly tag you if you aren't up for a snog. If NO comes into your head, you are just not ready, comfortable, or in the right situation or maybe he just ain't your type at all, girl.

angel + DEMON

(But to be laughed about as well as taken seriously on many occasions)

WHO, WHAT, WHEN, WHY, WHERE and HOW — saucy secrets

Sex can be awful, embarrassing, painful, boring, fun, amazing, dirty, slow, fast, average, sweaty, weird and many other things

Never feel out of control or uncomfortable. It is supposed to be fun! At the beginning it's normal to be nervous, to have the light off, and to fumble and mumble a bit. If after a while you're not feeling it, you're with the wrong boy. Don't worry, we've all been there.

You may not be comfortable about a boy doing this but it. Don't be a Prude, you definitely enjoy it if he do it well! Wax your bikini line too, as it is more likely he'll do a good job!

MASTURBATION

Some people do it, others don't. You're not weird if you do or don't. It takes a while to figure it out. Make it fun. Go to a sex shop — they have lots of crazy toys. It is true that every girl should own a dildo.

There are of books Don't be Find new you're doing spend a find sex too comfo and keep

There are so many ways to do it. Some are easy, some are not. Some you will prefer, some are impossible, some are boring, some are just naughty.

stroking — mov with he Move up then qu tickle hi Remember time so

Make sure you don't grip too hard, that you don't squash his nuts and that you make him feel sexy and not embarrassed. Ma sure you feel comfortable an sexy too. Play, tease an be mysterious.

You may never have one, you might get them all the time. They feel amazing. You have more of them if your boy hits the right spot, if it's important to him and if you're both enjoying yourselves. Do not fake them.

They are easy to catch. There are plenty of them flying around. They are easy to Prevent. Many of them are easy to spot. If he likes you he will use a condom until you both know that neither of you have them — a quick test at your local doctor is not too much to ask

Many girls don't like giving these, others do. Boys love them. There is no correct way of doing it, just learn what they like. Only do it if you know he has no STDs. Use a condom and only give one if you want to. Boys tend to ask for them — eeeww! It is definitely not ask and you shall receive, it's all good things come to those who wait.

Tara says get drunk and jump on someone. I say pick the guy you want and win him over. You feel pretty confident if you manage to seduce him. Don't be too obvious, but you have to make yourself known and make your interests clear. There is nothing more frustrating than being a really good friend if you really fancy him. Be funny. Talk about something you know will interest him, having done a bit of homework on what he likes. Chill out and be yourself. There is nothing worse than being tongue-tied and saying something really geeky. But then again he might find it really funny and be feeling just as nervous as you. That is what you have to remember — that he probably feels just as embarrassed and as much of a weirdo as you do. Be mysterious, chat to him for a while and then leave him thinking about you for a couple of days.

Do not tell a guy he is crap in bed. Things take time and you will really smash his ego, pride, sex drive, etc. He will probably never want to see you again. Show him how you like it, work on it. If you still are not enjoying it then you just aren't compatible. If there is no foreplay and he is a 'wham bam thank you mam' kind of guy — God, I sound like some Texan cowgirl! — find the nicest possible way to explain that you don't get turned on by that and ask if you can try something different. Or just take control of the situation girl, and make it up as you go along!

MIRROR, MIRROR ON THE WALL

WARNING: some days are bad hair days, others, it's skin. Others, you just feel fat and ugly.

BUT: A little piece of advice

NEVER FORGET TO LIKE WHAT YOU SEE SOMETIMES. FEEL SEXY – IT'S AN AMAZING FEELING – TAKE PRIDE IN HOW YOU LOOK AND WHO YOU ARE.

YOU ARE THE FAIREST OF THEM ALL...

1. You are unique. There is no one else like you, so make the most of it. You will spend your whole life finding out about yourself, and just when you think you know who you are your life will change and you will need to look after No. 1, as they say, and it will be your main responsibility in life. Keep your eyes open and don't do things the little voice in the back of your head is saying no to. You can always get away or run if you are in a situation where something doesn't feel right. The only person that really knows you is you.

...you think you hate, turn out to be totally the opposite. Be willing to accept your judgement was wrong... So my beautiful ballerina, actress, poet, writer, artist, scientist or mathematician, whatever you become, find some way of doing it, and may you always be happy.

2. You can be what you want, and wherever you want, and you can always change your mind. Reinvent yourself in new situations if you need to take a different approach. Don't listen to others who patronise, criticise and don't treat you the way you would treat them. Don't put up with being second best because you only disappoint yourself, your heart will tell you what you want in life at some point, even if it takes lots of things, doing things you like and being confused many times over. Try your hardest in life at some... hate and you will never regret anything. Try your hardest in both things you hate, just like people...

GORGEOUS GLAMOUR GIRL

DO NOT:

* Pick spots
* Use soap on face
* Sleep with make-up on
* Shave... (get a wax)
  (only in emergencies)

MAKE-UP

Use as many organic products as possible because your skin is like a sponge and soaks up chemicals — pretty gross, huh?

Blusher

Eyeshadow brush

Eyelash comb

Tweezers

Eyeshadow applicator

10 THINGS
a girl's handbag should contain

1 Lip gloss
2 Waterproof mascara
3 Nail file
4 Scent atomiser
5 Eyeliner & eyeshadow
6 Eyelash curlers
7 Blusher (light)
8 Tweezers
9 Moisturiser with SPF
10 Vaseline

BEAUTY SECRETS

MORNING

* Wash!
* Put on moisturiser. Buy a good expensive one, the more natural the better.
* Use a waterproof mascara.
* Eyeliner if you feel like it, just to line the eyes. A soft colour like khaki for green eyes.

(I only put eyeliner from the outer eye to half way, not whole lid. It makes your eyes look bigger)

EVENING

* Always start again.
* Do not wear make-up from day.
* Apply darker eyeliner, lighter shadow, or something sparkly.
* Use sharp but soft pencils. Use an eyeshadow brush. Don't colour whole eye, be subtle. Subtle = sexy. Put mascara on last and a tiny bit of blusher. I practise in a mirror.

BEFORE BED

* Take make-up off.
* Cleanse and tone.
* If you are wearing waterproof mascara, which I always do, use Vaseline on cotton wool to take it off. DO NOT USE OILY CREAMS, ETC. WITH ALCOHOL IN.

WASHING FACE

If you have spots, use a good face wash. Don't use a strong face scrub that contains alcohol — your skin will dry out. Only use a scrub three times a week.

TIPS

Pluck eyebrows underneath only & shape them.
Get a free makeover. Ask them to teach you how to use make-up and what colours suit you.
Lip gloss, sticky but sexy — always good.
Do not use harsh products. Use cotton wool to take make-up off.

SMOKY EYES

Thin line of liquid eyeliner
White undercoat.
Dark grey eyeshadow
Black mascara
Practice makes perfect.
Have cotton buds handy!

PRACTICE MAKES PERFECT

White eyeliner on lids close to eyelashes. Then copper sparkle eye shadow on top and underneath along bottom lids. I sometimes put a bit of sparkle on the inner corner. Looks exotic! With green eyes this looks wicked.

TIGER EYES

PURPLE HAZE

Light lilac + pink undercoat.
Slightly darker purple on outer eyelids. Not too much. Keep it subtle.

Eyes come in all shapes and sizes. Make sure your make-up goes well with your eye shape and your skin and hair colour. Halloween is only once a year and Goths are out! Less is more.

Khaki eyeliner. Light green undercoat. Mac does an amazing khaki kohl and sparkly green eye shadow. Black mascara.

CAMOUFLAGE

29

BAD HAIR DAY

Find a hairdresser you trust. Explain exactly what you want and go easy on the first cut. Don't be afraid to speak your mind if they are still cutting off too much. Lots of dye is bad. Lots of fringe & none off the back you may regret... yum, mullets.
Go easy on the blonde or you will look very pale. Pay a bit extra.
Do not copy a haircut from a magazine. You'll never look like the model in the picture.

GOOD BRUSH FOR CURLS

ALL THE GOOD CUTS I'VE HAD LOOKED TERRIBLE AT FIRST, BUT WITHIN TWO WEEKS LOOKED JUST RIGHT.

Use the right products.
Learn how to use a hairdryer (first few attempts you will feel badly coordinated).
Pick dyes close to your colour and streak (don't do whole head).
Choose an easily manageable cut.
Use hair straighteners only on bad hair days as they do dry hair out.

ACCESSORIES

Recipe to make
old clothes look new...

Big belts and small belts, bangles and shoes,
earrings and bracelets, a necklace or two.
Handbags or clutch bags, purses and jewels,
hats or a hairband, scarves or a shawl.

Gold shoes and gold belt,
black patent with red.
If your hair looks a mess,
put a hat on your head.

Match a belt and a bag
to your shoes and your skirt.
Mix a necklace and earrings,
add some lipstick to flirt.

slinky
bags

People stare at
red shoes. They always look good.

CLOTHES

Wear what you want to wear, match your crazy clothes, colours & hair

Create your very own style, but it may take a while!

Wear COLOURS

You can spot fashion no-no's a mile away

Be inventive, Be creative
It usually turns out
funky and different

GIRLS COMMENT
ON WHAT YOU'RE
WEARING WHEN IT'S
BAD OR WHEN THEY'RE
JEALOUS OR IF THEY
LOVE YOUR STYLE

FASHION NO-NO's

NEVER wear heels you can't walk in.

IF IT NEEDS IRONING, just do it.

DO NOT OVERSTATE make-up. Less is always more. Wrong colour foundation looks orange and awful.

TROUSERS that are too short look weird.

GRANNY PANTS — ARGHHH.

DON'T wear colours that don't suit you.

DON'T mix too many patterns.

34

FASHION YES YES YES's...

SEXY UNDIES always make a girl feel good. So do colours that flatter your skin and hair.

PICK OUT THINGS that other people wear and make them look better & more original on you.

IF YOU SEE something to die for try it on. Then go to a few more shops and if it's still on your mind, BUY IT.

BE COMFORTABLE in what you wear but sometimes wear things you never thought you would.

Accessorise.
Belts, handbags, jewellery. Buy cheap things off the internet. Train yourself to be a bargain hunter.

Wear sexy undies mmm...

Cotton stops you sweating in all areas, if you get what I'm saying! Look after your clothes — read washing instructions. Turn jeans inside out to wash.

Style is something personal. You are representing you and your personality through what you wear. Don't be a sheep. Dig out old clothes you've not worn for ages — things go in and out of fashion. Add a personal touch.

Make sure you get your bras properly fitted. They measure you in all good department stores. A bra that doesn't fit can be dangerous. White underwear is as sexy as black — if it's clean! Red can look tacky and cheap. It really depends on where you buy your underwear.

33

SHOP TILL YOU DROP

THIS IS AN OPPORTUNITY TO CHANGE YOUR LOOK. FIND OUTFITS YOU LIKE IN MAGAZINES, GO TO THE SHOPS AND IMPROVISE. BE CRAZY. TRY THINGS ON YOU NEVER IN A MILLION YEARS WOULD THINK SUITED YOUR STYLE THAT IS HOW YOU CHANGE YOUR LOOK. TAKE A FEW RISKS!

YOU FEEL PRETTY GOOD IF YOU PICK UP A COUPLE OF 'GOOD FINDS'

I SAY BUY LESS & SPEND MORE

1. It's better quality
2. It's usually more original and you wear it for ever.

A few good pairs of jeans do not go amiss. Maybe some sexy dark blue drainpipes you can turn up or wear with boots or heels.

Wear what you feel comfortable in, but get a slinky skirt and top. Dressing up in something sexy to go out in is so much fun.

A pencil skirt always looks sophisticated. Buy a couple of sexy black tops. If you are having a bad clothes day they always come in handy.

Keep a couple of funky colourful skirts you can wear day or night, summer or winter. Sexy hold-up stockings are always good.

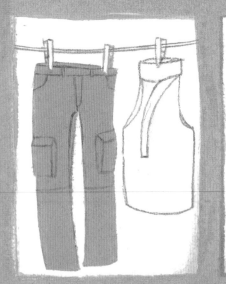

Colourful well-cut clothes that look smart and sophisticated make you feel so good. You'll look confident and successful and you will go a long way.

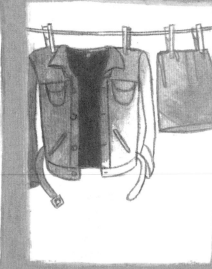

A girl should feel amazing in her clothes.

Organise your cupboards. It's easier to see what you have, what matches, what doesn't fit, and colour coordination is trouble free. You could divide your wardrobe up into work, party and play.

Change your look. You can be anyone you want to be: 60s chic, 70s girl, burlesque dancer, business woman, cowgirl. Combine outfits. Add a belt, hat, necklace, match your accessories. Vintage shops are perfect for finding different looks.

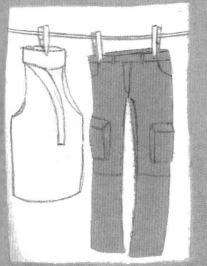

Read some magazines. Look at what is in for winter or summer, grab a friend and go to cheap shops, sales, charity shops and outlet stores. Some bargains might smell a bit musty, but nothing you can't wash out.

Use your imagination and good taste. Have the patience to look through all the hilarious rubbish or the boring sale rails where everything looks the same. You might find something cheap and perfect for your outfit.

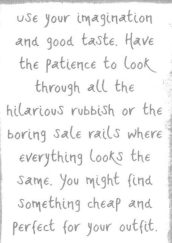

Lay your outfits out. Plan what you are going to wear. A last-minute rush is a nightmare. You ruin your make-up, you get hot and bothered, and the more you change the uglier and fatter you feel and the more frustrated you become.

The best thing about parties is coming home drunk & eating all the leftovers you can find in the fridge.

WHAT TO WEAR?

Wear shoes you can walk & dance in. You need to practise with stilettoes. Wear sexy clothes that are cool. Don't dress like a slut. People will laugh at you behind your back.

WHO TO GO WITH?

Go with your friends, people you know in case you need help. Go with people you trust not to go OTT & end up messing up your night. They are always the same people & they get tiresome.

WHAT TO DRINK?

You learn pretty quickly what alcohol you like and how much you can take. Don't drink fast and don't aim to get drunk at the start of a party or before you arrive. Remember the party lasts all night!

PARTY

It's pretty funny to be drunk with friends.

WHAT NOT TO DO?

Don't put your drink down where you can't see it or take drinks off people you don't know. Go to the bar with them to buy it if someone offers you a free drink.

WHERE TO STAY & HOW TO GET HOME?

Stay at a friend's house if you can't get home. Do not stay at a stranger's house. Don't let someone who has "only had a couple" drive you home – get a taxi.

WHAT TO BRING?

Bring a bottle of vodka to a party. It lasts longer, but don't drink the whole bottle.

WHEN TO SAY NO?

Don't get in a situation you can't handle because you are drunk. Anyone could take advantage of you & it's usually people you thought were nice & trustworthy. Don't take drugs.

WITH STYLE

IT'S ABOUT GOING OUT, having fun, getting tipsy, not spending too much money, dancing, laughing and chilling out.

A couple of drinks and you can dance without being nervous. A few too many and you look uncoordinated and really unattractive.

But sometimes it can end in tears...

39

It is good to be nervous about change, travel, exams, university and all the other new things that you have to do while growing up. It makes you who you are when you pluck up courage and do them and then wonder what you were being silly about.

Most things really do happen for a reason. It might not be immediately obvious, but when things happen that leave you wondering why, look at them positively.

Don't be a pushover. If there are certain things that you are not happy about decide what/who is not making you happy and tell them. Stand your ground.

WEIRD LITTLE THINGS

You will do or say things in life that may upset people. Listen to why — there are two sides to every story. Admit it if you were in the wrong.
You cannot please everyone all the time. You might have to say no or disagree with someone you think will take it badly. It usually turns out for the best.

YOUR BODY IS YOUR TEMPLE, DON'T FORGET IT. I didn't want to mention this. I know that this kind of stuff is extremely hard to talk about, so imagine how hard it is to write about. You never think that eating disorders will affect your life. You never think it could happen to you, or your best friend, or someone you love. Even the person affected by it rarely admits it or believes that they are actually wasting away and making themselves ill. If you are not eating, if you're throwing food away, making excuses for not being hungry, binge eating and then throwing up because you feel guilty, pushing your food around your plate, hate the sight of food and think that everything you eat is going to make you fat, READ THIS PAGE. You are not alone. People will understand you if you talk to them about it. You need to admit to yourself that you have a problem, which is extremely difficult, as usually you really believe that you are fine and in control. God, I sound like an irritating shrink. (Though even shrinks, counsellors, and psychologists can be helpful if it gets that bad. Try your friends and family first, though. They are usually pretty helpful and sympathetic.) You need to remember that the difficult times you go through in life are the most valuable ones. You can learn much more from having a tough time than from sailing through life, being the most popular chilled person with no problems. All the hard times I have had make me who I am. You learn from your mistakes as they say, and you can also help others who are in the same situation you were once in. OK let's get to the point.

THE MOST IMPORTANT THING IN LIFE

EATING OR NOT?
VOMITING?
DIETING?
PUNISHMENT?
ATTENTION?
ILLNESS?
HELP?
CONTROL?

Some people spend their whole lives dieting. Others are always teased for being stick thin or fat. You are what you are to a certain extent, and you should be happy with the way you look as long as you take care of yourself. The most awful thing I have ever had to watch was someone close to me push her food around the plate and not eat it, day in day out, as she got thinner and thinner. I was so unsympathetic towards people who have eating disorders because I couldn't understand what possessed them to even think about doing it to themselves. My questions were: why do you want to even make yourself ill? Why do you hate what you look like? How will you not eating solve the problem? Why are you trying to control your weight when you are not even fat? It is clear to me now that an eating disorder can happen to anyone. So what can girlies do to make sure it doesn't happen? How can they get help?

42

There are plenty of ways to control your weight sensibly, and it is definitely not through denying your body a healthy nourishing diet. Exercise – some love it, some hate it. Some people are good at it and others have had bad experiences at school or no chance to play in any teams or enjoy it. We have all tried to get out of sport with the forged signatures and faking illnesses or by using the 'time of the month' excuse when it's swimming. When you go to university and drink a lot, and have no set times to do sport, you realise how important it is to get into a routine of exercising. Do something you enjoy doing. Don't jog if you hate it – you will just give up in the end. Do a dance class or kickboxing, or cycle to school if you are just around the corner. If it is less embarrassing, join a club out of school. The more you think about dieting and losing weight, the more you will crave chocolate and junk food and put on weight. Tell yourself you are not on a diet, and eat sensibly, not excessively. It sounds obscene, but try eating small amounts five times a day. If you are someone who is always hungry or needs to snack when you are bored, buy nuts and raisins and fruit. You will find that the less crap you eat the more your cravings for junk diminish.

...IS YOUR BODY.

I am so scared sometimes by the number of people who psychopathically try to control what they eat. They believe everything they read or what some lentil-and-chickpea-eating hippy has to say, even when they have not got the faintest clue about good staple diets. Learning what your body can and can't take is a life-long battle, even for those who are not so worried about what they consume. You really can't afford to take certain things out of your diet because someone told you it was bad for you, or you read some stupid book about what colour your poo should come out and how to starve yourself on tofu. To me this is another form of anorexia.

If you are a complete weight control addict, be sensible about it. You need to understand what a healthy diet should consist of, what good food is, what is bad for your digestion and what you should eat together to stay alive and healthy. Find out what quantities are necessary to stay alive and healthy.

43

It is so funny to hear all your stories, and your worries about boys and teachers and trying to fit all your classes in! The older you get, the more work they pile on. But, the wiser you get, the more interesting life is. You actually realise that studying gets easier, especially when you find out what you are really interested in.

I am always nagging you to not leave stuff till the last minute, and to manage your time well. Maybe I just can't remember how chaotic school was. Do your work when it's given to you. Do it when it is still fresh in your mind. Last minute.com is like a high-risk sport — dangerous, fast and you can end up having a near fatal accident! It means: losing marks, high stress levels, not much respect from your teachers, and feeling like you could have and should have done better.

GCSEs are: your first big exams. They are pretty scary, but you need them so take them seriously. You have to revise and actually remember loads of pretty useless information! You have to start thinking about what subjects you might like to take for your A-levels.

OOOOOH my favourite part!
You remember when we spoke after your first week of lower sixth and I thought you sounded down? I said how weird sixth form was. You spend a normal summer, well, apart from waiting for your GCSE results. You go back to school and suddenly you are meant to be an adult, or you feel like something should have changed or has and you can't quite put your finger on it? The teachers treat you differently, you have fewer subjects, but more work. You are supposed to have loads of free periods, you have to manage your own time, but you realise you have less time. Why does it feel so weird? Well, you realise you are actually the same, nothing has changed but something makes you feel like everything should have changed!

SCHOOL
...THE PLACE WE LOVE TO HATE.

It is all very confusing. You all become amazing friends. A lot of the bitchiness dies down as people grow up and realise they are not the coolest people on earth. You all get quite nostalgic that you will all be leaving soon. There is a certain kind of life-long bond between people who have spent so much time together. Also, the girls who may not have been so sexy before, start looking much more interesting. Watch this space, girl. You definitely have an amazing two years ahead!

44

STUDENT SURVIVAL MANUAL

Moving out of home is pretty hard to get your head round. Especially if little people like you are still there being spoilt! You feel like you are deserting your family a bit. And there are no rules. You can go to bed when you want, eat what you want, leave as much stuff as possible lying around and generally rebel against everything you have ever been taught. Being a student is so much fun!

THERE ARE SOME DISADVANTAGES.

You are usually pretty tired, pretty unhealthy and your room ends up smelling, looking like a bomb's hit it and your life can generally be turned upside down.

WHAT'S MY ADVICE ON MOVING OUT OF HOME?

Do it. It is amazing and you need to become independent. You need to live with other people. You need to get away from your family, not for good, but for enough time to become yourself.

* If you are a pretty capable person, understand that not everyone will be as good as you at cooking or as schizophrenic about cleaning. Be reasonable and diplomatic, unless you are living with pigs.

* Make sure you live with people you like, or get along with! Well, I don't know actually. You could end up getting on better with the strangers in your house than the people you thought were your friends. * Accept people's weird little habits. Or try to at least.

* Have another group of friends to go out with. Better still, if they live close to you, you can pop round from time to time to escape crazy housemates. Join a couple of interesting societies - wine society, kickboxing, Spanish society.

* Get used to sharing everything, even other people's disgusting habits! Live with like-minded people who don't like living in squalor and actually like having a decent dinner together.

* Watch out for landlords. They are daylight robbers, difficult and usually pretty unreasonable. They like keeping your deposit, even if you leave the house how you found it.

Make sure you know what money is coming in and out of your bank. Check your statements. Look after your cards. Keep the bank telephone numbers safe, so that you can cancel your cards if your wallet gets lost or stolen. Don't keep your pin in your wallet with your cards either. Some stupid daddy's girl did that at uni and got a hell of a lot of cash stolen. She also didn't know how many cards she had, or how much money daddy was putting in her account, or how to cancel the cards, or even how to phone the bank. She just cried about her Tiffany key rings. You have to learn to look after your affairs and your parents should definitely fill you in. If not you will learn the hard way.

BORING BITS LIKE BANK ACCOUNTS AND BILLS.

Bills will come through your letterbox or out of your bank account all the time and they can be pretty large and a lot of the time they are confusing.

I took out a standing order with my bank to pay my landlord and didn't know I had to cancel it when I moved out of the house. The bank carried on paying him until I found out and it was pretty hard to get my money back.

Do not be the one to pay all the bills. Either set up a joint house account which you all put money into every month or collect all the money and give it to the person willing to write the cheque. Pay all your bills at the post office.

46

RULE NO.1

Never cook for people you don't like. It pisses me off when I have to share my food with people I don't want to talk to.

RULE NO.2

Dinners are the best times shared with friends.

WELL, YOU KNOW I HAVE TO PUT IN A SECTION ON COOKING...

RULE NO.3

You don't have to have a big repertoire, but you find if you can cook a few things a new recipe is usually easy to follow.

RULE NO.4

Teach yourself to be able to cook well enough so that you can look in a fridge, whether it's full, half full or practically empty, and make a meal out of what you have. You will never go hungry.

WHAT TO STOCK IN YOUR CUPBOARDS

Tomatoes are great for everything — sauces, stuffing, roasting, salads, sandwiches. I always keep some in my fridge.

Lemons are always useful. They go in a lot of things too — puddings, hummus, guacamole. Lemon granizado with a bit of vodka is an amazing cocktail: blend ice, lemon juice, alcohol, sugar and a bit of peel. Try lemon risotto, lemon with fish or chicken, lemon juice on salads.

Carrots can be roasted, put in a soup with coriander, in sauces for pasta, or just raw in a salad

It is always nice to have colourful veg.

You should eat at least five veggies a day

I buy vegetables every week and I try to alternate and buy different types each week so I don't get bored. Don't cook vegetables to death! They can go into practically anything raw or cooked. If they start to get old, make a soup.

Onions are a base for sauces, stews, stocks, roasts, rice, stir-fry, soup, bolognese, absolutely everything. I always buy a lot of onions. And whatever onion goes in, garlic does too. Red onion is a bit sweeter and less strong. Shallots (babies) are good roasted whole, in a stew or raw and finely chopped in salads.

Mushrooms are good in pasta sauces with some cream. They are cheap too. NEVER WASH THEM, GIVE THEM A WIPE.

Aubergines are so good. Try them roasted with other veg or in a Moroccan stew served with couscous.

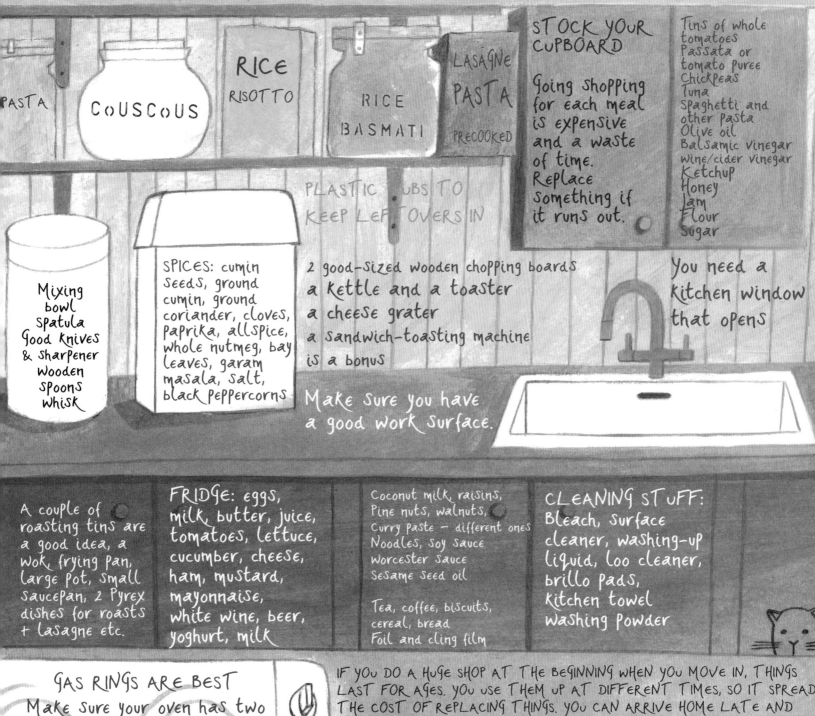

WHEN YOU GET A HOUSE...
There will be fewer fights if you and your housemates stock up and share most of the things on this page.

PASTA

COUSCOUS

RICE RISOTTO

RICE BASMATI

LASAGNE PASTA PRECOOKED

STOCK YOUR CUPBOARD

Going shopping for each meal is expensive and a waste of time. Replace something if it runs out.

Tins of whole tomatoes
Passata or tomato puree
Chickpeas
Tuna
Spaghetti and other Pasta
Olive oil
Balsamic vinegar
wine/cider vinegar
Ketchup
Honey
Jam
Flour
Sugar

PLASTIC TUBS TO KEEP LEFTOVERS IN

Mixing bowl
Spatula
Good knives & sharpener
Wooden spoons
Whisk

SPICES: cumin seeds, ground cumin, ground coriander, cloves, paprika, allspice, whole nutmeg, bay leaves, garam masala, salt, black peppercorns

2 good-sized wooden chopping boards
a kettle and a toaster
a cheese grater
a sandwich-toasting machine is a bonus

Make sure you have a good work surface.

You need a kitchen window that opens

A couple of roasting tins are a good idea, a wok, frying pan, large pot, small saucepan, 2 Pyrex dishes for roasts + lasagne etc.

FRIDGE: eggs, milk, butter, juice, tomatoes, lettuce, cucumber, cheese, ham, mustard, mayonnaise, white wine, beer, yoghurt, milk

Coconut milk, raisins, pine nuts, walnuts, curry paste — different ones
Noodles, soy sauce
Worcester sauce
Sesame seed oil

Tea, coffee, biscuits, cereal, bread
Foil and cling film

CLEANING STUFF: Bleach, surface cleaner, washing-up liquid, loo cleaner, brillo pads, kitchen towel washing powder

GAS RINGS ARE BEST
Make sure your oven has two shelves that you can take out and a grill

IF YOU DO A HUGE SHOP AT THE BEGINNING WHEN YOU MOVE IN, THINGS LAST FOR AGES. YOU USE THEM UP AT DIFFERENT TIMES, SO IT SPREADS THE COST OF REPLACING THINGS. YOU CAN ARRIVE HOME LATE AND KNOW YOU HAVE AT LEAST SOMETHING TO COOK. YOU CAN MAKE ANYTHING TASTE GOOD IF YOU HAVE A FEW SPICES. YOU FEEL WAY MORE CHILLED IF THERE IS FOOD IN THE HOUSE!

RICH BITCH

Don't let anyone take advantage of you, sneer at you or look down at you. Stand your ground.

THE TRICK IS TO ALWAYS HAVE ENOUGH MONEY SAVED TO DO THE THINGS YOU WANT. SOME MONTHS GO WITHOUT ANYTHING AND THE NEXT MONTH GO CRAZY. MANAGE YOUR MONEY WELL. SAVE FOR THINGS YOU REALLY WANT. BUY ONE EXPENSIVE THING INSTEAD OF SOMETHING CHEAP IF YOU KNOW YOU WILL WEAR IT A LOT. BUY OTHER CHEAPER THINGS THAT LOOK GLAM AND EXPENSIVE EVEN IF THEY AREN'T. YOU CAN DEFINITELY TELL THE DIFFERENCE IN A PAIR OF EXPENSIVE JEANS — THEY FIT BETTER AND LAST LONGER.

Talking about money and flaunting it is such bad manners. Be generous, but not overly as people usually try and take advantage of you. Never a borrower, never a lender as mama always told me, except in extreme circumstances. I have borrowed in the past and am so worried about paying it back on time, that I would rather not have the worry. Money and friends never go well together either.

Spend a day creating in the kitchen and have a few friends to dinner. Or find somewhere cheap that does good food, go out to dinner and enjoy yourself.

Get a cheap massage or your legs waxed or a manicure at least once a year. Save up and treat yourself. I always go for a wax.

Go out with the girlies for a glass of wine. I go every Thursday after work. It's so much fun to de-stress and giggle!

WOMEN'S SECRETS — how to spoil yourself

Go shopping on your own sometimes. You don't feel rushed and you always find the best stuff. It's pretty therapeutic.

Get the girlies in for the evening, curl up on the sofa and enjoy a good movie together with a few bottles of wine.

Go to a gallery or see something interesting. Sometimes I get there and wonder what I'm doing, but it gets you doing/seeing new things and motivates you to go on adventures.

LIKE MOTHER LIKE DAUGHTER

It is difficult being a mother as far as I can see. It is definitely difficult being a daughter. Sometimes you need to put yourself in your mum's shoes, and sometimes you need to remind her to remember what it was like.

Your mum shouts at you and you think that she is being unreasonable. Sometimes you tell her something that you wish you hadn't. Sometimes she punishes you and you think that she is just being mean. She is usually being hard on you for your own good.

You wish that she was like your friend's mum. You wish she treated you like a friend. You wish that you could make her proud, but you don't know how!

We often take our mothers for granted. I'm sure that they're trying to do what's best for us. Sometimes they get it wrong too. They're allowed to, but we are quick to let them know what they've done wrong, and sometimes we don't say it in the best of ways. Mothers and daughters will always have conflicts. What's difficult is finding a way to work through them. What is weird is that sometimes you can have the best day in the world with your mum, usually shopping, and then the next day you have some stupid row for nothing. Most of the time you don't even know why you're fighting and you hear yourself say awful things you wish you weren't saying. Mothers also have a knack of saying something like, "you are only nice to me when I buy you things", which does not help!

Mums see us making the same mistakes as they did and get a bit angry that they can't really stop us. They don't tell us that they did the same kinds of things. It must be hard to sit back and watch your daughter grow up, and it's hard to find the perfect balance between protecting her and letting her be independent. We think we're invincible, and we can be pretty rude and disrespectful. Parents are responsible for you. If anything happens to you, or if you fail in life, how do you think your parents are going to feel? Also, it is a scary prospect — you growing up and moving out of home. One minute the house is full of noise, laughter and people, and the next you are off to work, university or to travel and 18 years of devotion to your children goes like that. You are at home alone. Pretty scary don't you think?

Apologise and recognise that you have done something wrong. **1**

Don't lie about stuff. Your parents will be much more reasonable if you show that you are sensible and if you earn and maintain their trust and respect. **2**

Listen to what they have to say. You might not agree with all of it, but some of it usually makes sense. **3**

Spend some time together. You spend loads of time with your friends and then wonder why you get on better with them than you do with your mum (or daughter for that matter — mums can do the same). It takes time to build a relationship. **4**

Ring each other up. If you have left home, imagine how your mum is feeling. She may be having an amazing time without you, but there are some lonely times too. I bet she misses you. Even if you have had a row, ring her and chat about other stuff. Pretend it hasn't happened! **5**

Remember, she did exactly the same as you, had the same problems, worries and made the same mistakes. **6**

Let her know what's going on in your life. It is another story if she is just not interested.

Treat her like you treat your friends. If you aren't happy with the way they behave, I am sure you let them know, so let your mum know how you feel. **7**

Don't disagree for the sake of disagreeing. It's pointless. I bet you aren't nearly as argumentative with your friends. Or, is it because your mum is saying stuff you think you don't need or don't want to hear. Sometimes it is best to let her rant. **8**

Don't do stupid things that your parents would be disappointed in. They usually know exactly what you're up to. I'm not saying don't rebel a little bit. We all need to learn from our own mistakes. **9**

Remember, your family will always be your family, no matter what. So, as much as you fight, always make up. Try not to overstep the line. We sometimes go a bit too far because we know our family has to forgive us. It's difficult trying to keep everyone happy. Just make an effort. Forgive and forget hurtful things they might have done and enjoy each other. Life is too short. **10**

53

NASTY HABITS and more.

SMOKING: Well, I have smoked a fair bit. I know you hate it. So do I really, but from time to time a ciggie can be nice, especially with a glass of wine. But it's revolting. Look at old women smoking. It is the most unattractive sight ever. Try it, but don't get hooked. You don't want to get ill, smell of smoke the whole time, crave nicotine, etc. It is pretty disgusting. I started because I thought it was cool. It really is not!

CHEWING GUM: One thing I can't bear — the most unattractive, rank, gross, makes me feel sick habit — is girls chewing gum at 100 mph with their mouths open. Don't do it. You look soooo stupid chomping away, staring into space. Sorry, I had to put this in the book as it makes girls look so ugly.

THE EVIL EYE. Girls can give the nastiest looks sometimes. It may be unintentional, but watch out. Try not to look someone up and down too obviously, even if it is because you like their outfit. Sometimes someone's facial expression can be totally different to what they are thinking. I hate girls that look disapprovingly at me, it's awful. I know I do it without meaning to.

Mmm, bet you can't guess what this is? Thongs hanging out of the back of a pair of trousers are worse than looking at a builder's bum. I love thongs. They are the most comfortable underwear in the world. You don't have to pull your knickers out of your bum which is a pretty unattractive sight too. A thong stays where it should be usually, but sometimes it has a tendency to creep up out of girlies' jeans and be oh so visible. Please put it away, chicas!

THINGS THAT GO HORRIBLY WRONG!

I thought up this page when I missed my flight in Barcelona and my debit card stopped working. You will probably get into a few pickles in your lifetime, too, and not know what to do.

You get locked out of your car. You can call someone like the AA out for about 50 squids, but it is easier to keep a spare key somewhere safe.

You have a debt with the bank and they send you awful letters telling you that you're going to be blacklisted and that they are going to send the bailiffs round to take all your stuff. Go and see your bank manager. Usually it is not as bad as it seems. If you have a spare tenner, pay it into the bank. That'll keep them quiet for a while until you find a way to pay the money back.

Your credit or debit card does not work or gets swallowed by the machine. Go into the bank and report it. If the bank is closed, go back the next day, or call them and they will help you sort it out.

If you miss your flight, you can usually pay a penalty and book another one. Just don't get angry, flustered and upset. It is not worth it. Accept that these things happen and you will feel slightly calmer and less stressed out.

You have a work crisis and you have forgotten to do an essay, or you left it until the last minute and you are completely screwed. No, you are not. Do as much work as you can on it overnight and talk to your teacher. They are usually helpful and reasonable. Unless you do it all the time!

Remember: People are on your side. Be polite and you will usually be helped. Cry if you have to. You probably will be crying anyway if something bad has happened.

If you've got yourself into a tizz wozz and have no idea what to do, sit down and think what the best way out is. Take every situation as it arises, calmly and knowing that it really is not the end of the world, and that there must be a way to sort it out. Call someone. Your parents should be there any hour of the day — reverse charges if you are too skint to pay! Go to an advice desk. Call 999. It depends on what sort of trouble you are in. The funny thing is, disasters usually make a good story or life a bit more interesting.

Life usually has a few beauties in store for you. So, just stay calm, then it is much easier to figure out what to do next.

GEEKS ARE ORIGINAL...

BULLIES are usually cowards or just plain stupid. They may be having problems at home and at school, or they're trying to look cool in front of their mates. Not so long ago bullies just used to call people names. Now I can't believe how serious and aggressive bullying has become. Report bullies if they make your life hell. Don't listen to bullies. They are not worth it. Both you and I got picked on and I don't know about you, but I'd like to thank the stupid boys and girls that picked on me. They taught me how to stand up for myself, and how to take no notice. Watch out — teachers can be bullies too.

Kids at school label each other, and one of these stupid labels is GEEK. It's funny that we were both quite geeky at school. Well I know I was, and look how we turned out... pretty cool actually. We do our own thing, enjoy ourselves and always manage to do our work and have fun. You deal with nasty people in your own quiet way and I stood up for myself and got defensive and we have always done well at the things we like. We have learnt not to follow the crowd, we ignore people's comments and bitchy girls, and we probably have the best group of friends. You know your friends would stand by you because you are what you are, they like you very much and aren't with you to get a good reputation. Being a geek is amazing, interesting, hard work but worthwhile. I wouldn't be me, or enjoy being me if I wasn't a bit of a geek.

BULLIES ARE NOT

POPULAR GIRLS

are really nice if you are in their group. If you are not, they don't have the time of day for you. There are always going to be different bunches of people at school, and you should never think that you are lucky to be in a popular crowd. Yeah, OK, everyone wants to be like you, all the boys want to go out with you, everyone wants to invite you to their party. However, it's pretty tough when you leave school and your little clique of worshippers disappears. You are like a fish out of water. Popular girls are usually the least confident, very self-conscious and are actually pretty normal and boring compared to those that have to fight for their place in this world. Whatever group you are in, enjoy it and be nice to people who aren't in your gang.

SPORTY PEOPLE...

are just doing what they love and what they're good at. They're usually quite loud and lairy and go out and get plastered at university. Some of them are big scary meatheads, but some are extremely clever. Sporty people have an advantage... ready-made friends, playing in a team, a discipline, a hobby, and when they go to uni, they end up staying fit and not growing beer guts. Sport is scary at school, but even if you aren't good at it please play in some kind of team. It's really nice to do something other than homework and with a group of people who like doing the same thing as you.

BAD INFLUENCES,

smoking, drinking, getting wasted at parties is not fun if you are the person who has to lie to parents, clean up sick and take your friend to the family planning clinic for the morning-after pill. It's fun getting up to mischief, but most bad influences are not thinking about others around them or the consequences of what they are doing. They are selfish. They are usually a bit screwed up. The best thing to do is be as good a friend as you can be but not get caught up in everything that they are doing. Be their sane friend. If you are that bad influence, just think a little bit about what you are doing to yourself and to your mates and about how they feel too.

DON'T BE ASHAMED

of who you are or what crowd you're in. Just make sure you don't hurt other people. Don't bully people because of what they aren't or to make yourself look cooler. Use your brain and understand that the world is so big, people can't all be in the same tribe. We are all different. Enjoy your group of friends. Don't put down others who have their own gang. Tell your friends you don't like their behaviour if they do something wrong or say when something hurts you or someone else. If you are afraid to stand up to one of your friends, then they really are not a good buddy, are they? Stand up for yourself. Be original, don't follow the crowd. Find something that you like doing, maybe something you wouldn't usually sign your name up for. Have a couple of sets of friends. Don't put other people down because they are different from you. Enjoy the fact that no one is the same and you never know — you might one day need to count on someone and the only person who is around is someone you picked on. Don't do it. It is not nice and it reflects badly on you.

PEOPLE

BE FLY be your own person

let bitchy stuff go in one ear and out the other

Do not take shit from anyone. Stand up for yourself and what you believe in.

You will make friends and break friends and lose them naturally through outside occurrences that you cannot control. Keep your friends close and your enemies closer, as they say! You will also change and not spend so much time with people you imagined you'd see every day forever. Just keep a good group of friends who you know you can totally rely on.   If people make you feel bad about yourself, walk away. It's not worth feeling uncomfortable, just to be in with the so-called 'cool' people.

People are very strange and diverse. People behave in very bizarre ways. Some people have strong opinions, big personalities and are independent, confident and strong willed. Other people are nervous or cagey. Some people think that they need to be someone they aren't. They are usually false try-hards. Some people are real, down to earth, kind hearted and honest. Spend time with lots of different types of people. Learn how to deal with the difficult ones and the annoying ones. Watch people, use your instincts and take time to determine what people are like before you become their friend. I think spending time with weirdos, bitchy girls, brash, arrogant and rude people helps you understand how to deal with nasty people. Smile politely, always be nice and always protect yourself. Being genuine gets you far.

BELIEVE IN YOURSELF

I was going to use this picture to remind you that you are sexy and to never stop feeling it, but the picture underneath is better. Please lift the flap.

DRUGS ARE:

An extremely large part of growing up. A lot of your friends will take them, offer them to you and think they are the dog's bollocks because they got a bag of coke or a couple of pills for a party.

Unpredictable. Other friends will get ill, get manic depression, have horrendous accidents, and die from using drugs.
My advice is, play with fire and you will get burned. You never know what chemicals are in drugs and usually they are cut with the most unpleasant things... best not to get involved.

Exciting to talk about, but boring after a while. They won't improve your night and definitely not your life or your personality.

Dangerous and not so cool.
I would never in a million years recommend that you try them. Don't be swayed by peer pressure. Saying 'NO', making your own decisions in life and not copying the crowd will gain you a lot more respect from your friends.

For people who can't make their own fun and are sad losers with no personality trying to prove something or trying to be cool. Being high on illegal substances is really not the best way to spend your cash or your night!

Mushrooms

Ecstasy

Coke

LSD

Weed

Hash

Mushrooms are hallucinogenic, they distort your perception of everything and, although they are natural, they are still illegal.

Ecstasy makes you feel loved up. You want to dance and you are happy. But you can get a bad one. You can lose the plot and the next day you can't do anything. Come downs are bad. You never want to experience them.

Coke is really not attractive. It makes you talk absolute rubbish, gives you insomnia, can permanently damage your nose and turns you into the most selfish animal imaginable.

LSD makes you hallucinate. It is extremely strong and can have the most terrible effects while taking it and in the long run.

Weed and hash make you stoned and sleepy. Some people can smoke it, others can't. Some people get serious paranoia.

Be motivated.
Be enthusiastic. Use your talents.
If you have a dream, make it happen.
Be resourceful. Recycle and make
the most of what you have.

Life is about staying out of trouble,
and enjoying yourself at the same time.
It is about survival, being kind, earning
respect and being trustworthy. So
behave yourselves, girls!

Look after your
friends and family.
They are extremely
important. Being nice
to people gets you
a long way.

THE WORLD
is your oyster!

Follow the rules
or you will be left
behind. Go to school,
work hard and use
whatever opportunities life
throws at you in order to
be successful. I'm only just
realising now that getting
good grades and studying
a worthwhile course at
university is important.
If you hate studying, find
a trade, stick to it and
make yourself employable.
Money is not the answer
to everything but it
is useful.

Life is about
instincts and common
sense. If it doesn't come
naturally it is really
important to learn how to
be sensible, and about not
doing anything too stupid.
You are not invincible. Look
after your skin, your hair
and your body or you will
look like an old hag
by the age of 24!

Don't be afraid. We all
make our own luck in this world.
Those who fear life are never fulfilled.
You want to meet interesting people and
have interesting stories to tell them.
Hey, I wrote this book for my little
sister and it got published!

Most of all enjoy life.
Boys are fun, girls are fun, parties are
crazy and travelling is amazing. You want
to look back on life and be proud of what
you have achieved. Do not lead a boring life,
or a life full of mistakes and regrets.

IT'S A CLICHÉ BUT 'LIFE IS SHORT, DON'T WASTE IT'.

DO'S

WARNING: TAKING DRUGS CAN SERIOUSLY DAMAGE YOUR MIND AND YOUR BODY.

DON'Ts

Do always be sensible. I can't stop you from trying anything. We live in a world full of this stuff and I would be daft to deny it. Do call your sis before taking anything.

Do watch what happens to other people on drugs. Watch how they react. People usually behave like idiots on drugs so it is more fun to get a bit drunk and stay out of it.

Do leave a room or a party if you are not comfortable with what people are doing.

Do let people know if you have been stupid enough to take drugs. At least if something goes wrong, someone will know what you are on.

Do remember that drugs can permanently alter the chemical balance in your brain. I can guarantee you will see personality changes in those who abuse chemicals.

Don't be forced into anything.

Don't follow what others are doing to not feel left out.

Don't think just because everyone else keeps telling you it's amazing it's a good excuse to take something.

Don't believe people when they say you will be fine/they will look after you. They could have a bad trip/you could and they will not want to help. People are not themselves on drugs.

Don't think I am trying to preach to you. Remember there is a huge amount of advice on drug abuse floating around, and sometimes it denies the fact that in this day and age most kids try drugs at some stage of their life. Just understand that you only get one chance on this planet and you are not invincible.

In the advice above, I am under no circumstances trying to encourage the use of illegal substances. However, I was not born yesterday and nor were you. Stupid people offer, weak people try, and sensible people say 'no'. Just make sure that you don't screw up. Taking drugs is a dangerous game to play.